The First 90 Days of Sobriety

Recovering from Alcoholism

A GUIDED JOURNAL

DR. NATALIE FEINBLATT

ROCKRIDGE
PRESS

For general information on our other products and services or to obtain technical support, please contact our Customer Care Department within the United States at (866) 744-2665, or outside the United States at (510) 253-0500.

Rockridge Press publishes its books in a variety of electronic and print formats. Some content that appears in print may not be available in electronic books, and vice versa.

Interior and Cover Designer: Jane Archer
Art Producer: Hannah Dickerson
Editor: Adrian Potts
Production Editor: Sigi Nacson
Production Manager: Jose Olivera

Illustration © Fotini Tikkou, p. 62

ISBN: 978-1-64876-463-9
R0

Contents

Introduction

AS SOMEONE WHO IS LOOKING TO TACKLE your first 90 days without alcohol, you're probably experiencing many difficult and possibly conflicting thoughts, feelings, and physical sensations. Even in the face of all that, I want you to know you are capable of making the change you're thinking about, and I welcome you to this journey, which may be the most important one you will ever take.

Perhaps this is the first time you will be attempting to stay sober from alcohol for 90 days. It's also possible you have been down this road before and want to recommit to the path. Please know that this journal is designed to help with both sets of circumstances. Whether this is your first try or relapse is a part of your story, this book can be a support for you.

I'm Dr. Natalie Feinblatt, and I'm a licensed psychologist who has been working in addiction treatment for most of my 20-year career in the mental health field. I have supported hundreds of people recovering from alcoholism as they made their way through their first 90 days and beyond. I've also been on my own journey for many years, working to recover from compulsive behaviors that were harming me and those closest to me. I've gathered a lot of recovery experience along the way, and I wanted to create this guided journal as a way of sharing that wisdom with a group of people who need all the tools and coping skills they can possibly get.

During my time working in addiction treatment, I have never seen people look as accomplished and hopeful as they do when they make it to 90 days sober. Any amount of time sober is reason to celebrate, but there's something special about being able to string together 90 consecutive days. Relapse rates are at their highest during this time frame, so making it through that battle is truly a badge of honor.

This journal exists to help you take care of yourself and stay on track during the first 90 days of your sobriety. Recovering from alcoholism is not something you can do by yourself without any outside help or tools. As a matter of fact, thinking you can do it all on your own is a weakness, not a strength. It takes a tremendous amount of courage to accept that you need support with something like this.

You're going to need all the help you can get, so let this book be of assistance to you. People recovering from alcoholism tend to get stuck in their own heads. Their thoughts swirl around and around—cravings, insecurities, resentments, fears, plans, and more. Perhaps you even drank sometimes to quiet this noise. Journaling helps get that maelstrom out of your head and onto paper. It helps you clear your mind and organize your thoughts.

Each week, you will get a mixture of daily prompts and practices. Prompts will encourage you to write about certain ideas or issues you may be facing. Practices will give you something concrete to try outside the journal to add to your box of recovery tools. I have adapted these prompts and practices from my years of professional and personal experience with addiction recovery. Some of them are my own creations, and others pull from the wisdom of the peer support groups that sober people often attend. At the end of every week, there will be a check-in designed to help you focus on tracking aspects of your physical self-care during your 90-day journey.

As I have already mentioned, many people with alcoholism who try to get sober participate in peer support groups. The most well known is Alcoholics Anonymous (AA), but there are many others, including (but not limited to) SMART Recovery, Recovery Dharma, Celebrate Recovery, and Secular Organizations for Sobriety (SOS). My clinical opinion as an addiction professional is that participating in some sort of peer support group is essential to successful sobriety and recovery. I often tell my clients, "I don't care which one you go to, as long as you go to one!" However, this guided journal is designed for everyone, regardless of whether a peer support group is part of your recovery. You will find that the prompts and practices work both in conjunction with most peer support groups and independently of them.

Starting Your Recovery

If you have a problematic relationship with alcohol, the odds are good that you will experience some withdrawal symptoms when you stop drinking. Although many people don't have severe symptoms, those who have been drinking heavily over a long period of time may develop serious and medically dangerous symptoms. If you experience any of the following symptoms when you stop drinking, please contact a doctor immediately to discuss whether you need to detox under the care of medical professionals.

- Debilitating nausea and vomiting

- Extreme body tremors

- Severe sweating

- Strong anxiety and agitation

- Confusion and disorientation

- Hallucinations

Whether your withdrawal symptoms are mild or so significant that they need to be medically managed, you *can* get and stay sober. Use your experience with withdrawal symptoms as motivation to maintain sobriety, so you will never again have to return to this point in the journey.

The 90-Day Journal

Welcome to Sobriety

Every journey has to start somewhere, and here you are at the beginning of yours. Congratulations! Know that so many people never make it to this point, and you deserve to pat yourself on the back for arriving at this trailhead. Although you made the decision to be here, looking out at the road ahead may be overwhelming at first. That is understandable and very normal. To make it more manageable, write about one small positive thing you want to accomplish today. Maybe it's just to stay sober and literally nothing else—that's great! Whatever it is, spend some time reflecting on why it matters to you and how you will work to achieve it.

One Day at a Time

"One day at a time" is a very helpful slogan because thinking about being sober for the rest of your life is way too overwhelming for most newly sober people. It feels much more manageable to think about being sober just for today, and then deal with tomorrow when it comes. But perhaps a whole day still seems like too much for you. Can you stay sober one hour at a time? One minute at a time? What feels doable for you right now? Write about how you are going to spend your time so you can make it through the coming minutes, hours, and day sober.

_____

_____

_____

_____

_____

_____

_____

_____

Relapse Safety Plan

It's best to come up with a relapse safety plan ahead of time because if you do relapse, you won't be in the best head space to make healthy decisions. Remember, just because you're planning *for* a relapse doesn't mean you're planning *to* relapse. The prompts below are a useful starting point to map out your own safety plan. When you are done, share this plan with another person, because doing so will increase the likelihood that you will follow the plan if needed.

Once you've started drinking, how can you stop ASAP? (Ideas can include pouring any remaining alcohol down a sink, physically leaving the situation, and not giving in to the idea that because you've already relapsed, you might as well keep drinking.)

Who can you reach out to, to disclose the relapse and ask for help?

How can you strengthen your willingness to follow the directions given by those close to you?

_____

_____

_____

_____

_____

Where can you go to be safe and around other supportive people?

_____

_____

_____

_____

_____

Powerlessness

You're using this journal because you lost control of your drinking. You wanted to slow down or stop, and you tried a bunch of different ways to do it, but none of them worked. If you could control your alcohol use, you wouldn't be using this journal in the first place. What is the evidence that you are indeed powerless over alcohol? How is it actually empowering to accept your powerlessness over alcohol?

Baby Steps

There's nothing wrong with setting teeny tiny goals for yourself. As a matter of fact, it's a good strategy! You're more likely to achieve small goals, and those achievements help you build the self-esteem you need to set and achieve larger and larger goals. Think of a sobriety-related task and start to break it down into baby steps for yourself. List those baby steps below, and make them easily achievable. By hopping from baby step to baby step, you'll accomplish the end goal in no time.

Sample task: *I need to find a peer support group to attend tomorrow night.*

1. *Look up local meetings on my laptop.*

2. *Write down time and address of meeting.*

3. *Use GPS app to figure out what time I need to leave to get there a little early.*

4. *Set an alert on my smartphone.*

5. *And so on . . .*

My task:

The steps I will take:

The 5-4-3-2-1 Technique

It's easy to lose your bearings during early sobriety. Urges to drink, rampaging emotions, and so much change can knock you off-center. A good way to get grounded again is the 5-4-3-2-1 technique. You can practice it any time, either out loud or to yourself. It reorients you to your current place and time, helping you regain focus and clarity in the present moment.

→ What are 5 things you can see right now?

→ What are 4 things you can hear right now?

→ What are 3 things you can feel on your skin right now?

→ What are 2 things you can smell right now?

→ What is 1 thing you're grateful for right now?

This week I learned: _____

My biggest challenge was: _____

My biggest success was: _____

Self-Care Checklist

Y	N	
		Am I sleeping okay?
		Am I staying hydrated?
		Am I eating well?
		Am I moving around much?

TIP: *Alcohol dehydrated you, so make sure to drink plenty of water early on in sobriety. Generally speaking, you should drink one ounce of water per day for every pound you weigh.*

This Week I Have . . .

○ Connected with another person.

○ Thought of things I'm grateful for.

○ Been kind and gentle with myself.

○ Stepped outside my comfort zone.

○ Taken direction from someone who knows more than I do.

I am staying sober because:

_____

_____

_____

_____

_____

_____

_____

_____

_____

_____

Free Time

Many people in early sobriety find that they suddenly have a lot of free time on their hands. Sometimes it's because drinking took up most of their free time. Sometimes it's because they have lost relationships or even their job because of their addiction. Either way, a bunch of open time and the boredom it might breed can spell trouble for someone trying to stay away from alcohol. Are the openings in your schedule triggering you? What constructive activities can fill your newly found free time? What hobbies, activities, or relationships can you involve yourself more in? Start laying out a schedule of new habits and routines to fill your days.

Rationalizing

It's been over a week now. Is your disease trying to rationalize its way out of sobriety yet? At this point, the brains of most people with alcoholism are trying to convince them they aren't actually under the spell of alcoholism and they can drink again safely. It never got that bad, right? You can control it if you just try harder this time. Uh-oh, busted! If your brain is up to these tricks, call it out. Write about these rationalizations and why they are dead wrong based on evidence from your past.

_____

_____

_____

_____

_____

_____

_____

_____

_____

_____

Reaching Out

It's possible to get sober all on your own, but it's really difficult. It is much easier with a mixture of social, peer, and professional support. Today, contact one friend, one person who's also on a sobriety journey, and one helping professional you're working with. Just check in with them about how your day is going and the challenges and successes you're facing in this moment.

If you don't have one or more of these people, develop a plan for finding them. Is there a friend you can open up to? Is there a support group where you can meet other newly sober people? See the Resources section (page 110) for information about finding a therapist.

All the Feels

It is often said that if you want to find out why you're doing something, stop doing it. The odds are that in your early sobriety, a bunch of emotions you don't want to deal with are starting to come up. Remember, these feelings didn't disappear when you drank; instead, they hid and worked out so they could pop up even stronger when you got sober.

Write about the unwelcome feelings you're experiencing. What are they? Why were you trying to medicate them away? How can you begin to work to integrate them back into your life? Brainstorm three ways you can deal with these feelings more effectively next time they come up. Could you journal about them, share them with a friend, or let yourself cry it out?

Self-Compassion

Dr. Kristin Neff has developed a wonderful self-compassion practice to follow when you are experiencing any kind of suffering. If you are craving alcohol, contemplating relapse, or experiencing painful emotions that you would usually drink to numb, give this process a try.

1. Say out loud or to yourself, "This is a moment of pain." You can tweak the language if needed ("I'm struggling a lot right now," "Things are so hard," etc.).

2. Say, "Pain is a part of life." Again, you can adjust the language if you want ("Everyone experiences pain," "Pain is normal," etc.).

3. Say, "May I be kind to myself in this moment." Gently lay your hands on your heart, your cheeks, or anywhere it feels comfortable to do so. Comfort yourself with your own touch and continue to speak to yourself as you would to a friend or child. Say something like, "I'm so sorry you're going through this. It's going to be okay. I care about you a lot."

What was it like to try this self-compassion practice? What thoughts and feelings came up for you?

_____

_____

_____

_____

_____

HALT

Check in with yourself right now using the handy HALT acronym. Are you:

H **UNGRY?**
If so, eat something.

A **NGRY?**
If so, acknowledge, accept, and express the feeling in a healthy way.

L **ONELY?**
If so, reach out and connect with someone.

T **IRED?**
If so, get some rest.

Make a HALT check-in part of your daily routine. It often provides the answer to why you're feeling especially restless, irritable, or discontent. Plus, it's just good self-care.

This week I learned: _____

My biggest challenge was: _____

My biggest success was: _____

Self-Care Checklist

Y	N		
		Am I sleeping okay?	
		Am I staying hydrated?	
		Am I eating well?	
		Am I moving around much?	

TIP: *Alcohol impairs your body's ability to absorb nutrients, vitamins, and minerals. Try to "'eat the rainbow" of fresh fruits and veggies to renourish your body.*

This Week I Have . . .

○ Connected with another person.

○ Thought of things I'm grateful for.

○ Been kind and gentle with myself.

○ Stepped outside my comfort zone.

○ Taken direction from someone who knows more than I do.

I am staying sober because:

_____

_____

_____

_____

_____

_____

_____

_____

_____

_____

Trauma

Many people with alcoholism use alcohol to medicate away symptoms of post-traumatic stress. If that's the case for you, your trauma is probably starting to resurface in painful ways. Please know that this is normal and you are not alone. You can heal from trauma without using alcohol to numb the pain. Brainstorm ways you can get the help you need to cope with your past. How can you search for a trauma therapist? What books might be helpful to read? How can you find a trauma support group? Most people with alcoholism are also trauma survivors, so there are many resources out there, if you look for them. The Resources section on page 110 contains some useful starting points.

Change

Do you want things in your life to change without doing anything differently? Unfortunately, it doesn't work that way. Nothing changes if nothing changes—and in your case, *you* need to make changes in your life to stay sober. Aside from stopping drinking, what are three changes you are hoping to make in your life now that you're sober? What could get in the way of this process? How can you work to overcome those obstacles?

Bilateral Tapping

Bilateral stimulation (or BLS) helps your brain and body integrate information from the two hemispheres of your brain by alternately stimulating the left and right sides of your body. You can do so in a variety of ways, including touching or tapping. When it's done slowly, BLS can have a very calming and grounding effect.

To see if it works for you, give the butterfly hug a try. Cross your arms over your chest so your right hand touches your left shoulder and your left hand touches your right shoulder. Slowly alternate tapping your right and left shoulders for about one minute. If you find it calming, put BLS in your box of coping skills for the next time you feel out of sorts.

Pulling a Geographic

Many people with alcoholism fantasize about how their life will completely change for the better if they move to another city, state, or even country. This is known as "pulling a geographic," and it almost never works. The scenery may change, but you and your alcoholism are still there.

Spend some time writing about your experience with pulling a geographic. Have you only thought about it or have you actually tried it? What are you or were you hoping to change? What can you learn from this experience?

_____

_____

_____

_____

_____

_____

_____

_____

_____

Do This for You

Is getting sober truly your own desire, or are doing it to salvage a relationship with a loved one? No matter how much you love someone—a family member, partner, friend—your recovery will not last if you are doing it because of them. If sobriety is going to stick, you need to do it for you first and foremost.

Reflect on the reasons you might be getting sober for other people. Is there any way to repurpose these motivations so you are getting sober for yourself instead of for them?

Sleep Hygiene

Getting enough quality sleep is a challenge for many newly sober people. Sleep hygiene practices can help get your sleep back on track.

→ Set fixed times to go to sleep and wake up. Our bodies and brains respond well to this structure and routine.

→ Use your bed only for sleep. This habit strengthens the connection in your brain between your bed and sleeping.

→ Sleep in a quiet and dark room at moderate temperature.

→ Avoid caffeine and exercise for several hours before bedtime to give your body and brain sufficient time to wind down.

→ Develop a soothing pre-sleep routine. It can include a cup of herbal tea, light reading, listening to calming music, or similar activities.

→ If you can't sleep, don't toss and turn for more than 20 minutes. Get out of bed and do some relaxing activity in dim light (read, stretch, etc.) before trying to sleep again.

This week I learned: _____

My biggest challenge was: _____

My biggest success was: _____

Self-Care Checklist

Y	N	
		Am I sleeping okay?
		Am I staying hydrated?
		Am I eating well?
		Am I moving around much?

TIP: *Remember to try to implement some sleep hygiene tips from yesterday's practice to see if they help improve your sleep quality.*

This Week I Have . . .

○ Connected with another person.

○ Thought of things I'm grateful for.

○ Been kind and gentle with myself.

○ Stepped outside my comfort zone.

○ Taken direction from someone who knows more than I do.

I am staying sober because:

_____

_____

_____

_____

_____

_____

_____

_____

_____

_____

_____

A Greater Power

Many people recovering from alcoholism find it helps their sobriety to believe in a power greater than themselves. Some have a religious or spiritual belief, while others go in a more pragmatic or scientific direction. What power(s) do you believe in that is greater than yourself? How does this belief help you with your sobriety?

_____

_____

_____

_____

_____

_____

_____

_____

_____

_____

_____

Locus of Control

Making your sobriety dependent on the behavior of others can jeopardize your progress. Other people will do things that disappoint, upset, and hurt you. Others may even attempt to sabotage your sobriety. But ultimately, the decision of whether to drink in response to their behavior is in *your* hands.

How can you fight back against your alcoholism when it tells you that your sobriety lies in the hands of others? What are three constructive ways you can cope next time someone causes you distress? Coping strategies could include reading a statement you wrote for yourself ahead of time or calling a trusted friend to discuss the issue before taking any action.

Sensory Soothing Box

Make a box filled with items you can use to soothe your five senses. You can do this self-care practice on a small and inexpensive scale. Pull out the box when you are experiencing painful feelings as a way of showing yourself love and compassion. Items can include (but are not limited to):

→ **Sight:** A picture book, photos, or crayons to color with

→ **Touch:** A stress ball to squeeze, a spiky massage ball, or a soft cloth to rub on your skin

→ **Smell:** Essential oils, perfume, or incense

→ **Taste:** Herbal tea, hard candies, mints, or gum

→ **Sound:** A seashell to hold up to your ear, a white noise or nature sound machine, or a music box

And Then?

Cravings are a normal part of early sobriety. When you get the urge to drink, you usually think only about the immediate payoff of intoxication. It's a good idea to take the thought further by repeatedly asking yourself, "And then?" This is a great way to play the tape all the way through and see what will actually happen if you drink.

Example: "I'm going to drink and then I'll feel much better."
    And then?
    "And then I'll need to drink more to keep it up."
    And then?
    "And then I'll have to hide that I'm drunk so people don't find out."
    And then?
    "And then I'm going to lie to people about it so they don't know I relapsed."
    And so on . . .

Write out what this scenario would look like for you. Return to this practice any time you notice a craving.

_____

_____

_____

_____

_____

_____

It's Not a Big Deal

Many newly sober people become fixated on the idea that other people will pay a lot of attention to the fact that they are no longer drinking and may have a problem with it. The reality is that almost no one will care that you're not drinking anymore. Most people spend their time thinking about themselves, not you and your sobriety. But is there a reason you are so convinced they'll notice and take issue with it? What do you think this concern says about where you are with your sobriety? How can you stay focused on your journey no matter what others may (or may not) think?

_____

_____

_____

_____

_____

_____

_____

_____

_____

Self-Talk

Do you talk to yourself in a way that you would never speak to another person? If so, try this practice today. When you verbally berate yourself, stop and write down how you would speak to a beloved friend or a child in this situation. When you're finished, find a mirror and read out loud what you wrote. What feelings does it bring up for you? Can you turn this practice into a tool you can use to change your self-talk for the better?

This week I learned: _____

My biggest challenge was: _____

My biggest success was: _____

Self-Care Checklist

Y	N		
		Am I sleeping okay?	
		Am I staying hydrated?	
		Am I eating well?	
		Am I moving around much?	

TIP: *Instead of using exercise as a test of endurance or a means of changing (or punishing) your body, find types of movement you actually enjoy that make your brain and body feel good.*

This Week I Have . . .

○ Connected with another person.

○ Thought of things I'm grateful for.

○ Been kind and gentle with myself.

○ Stepped outside my comfort zone.

○ Taken direction from someone who knows more than I do.

I am staying sober because:

_____

_____

_____

_____

_____

_____

_____

_____

_____

_____

_____

Act as If

Sometimes early sobriety involves a bit of pretending. When you're not sure how to handle an issue, you can "act as if" you do. When you lack confidence in your ability to stay sober you can "fake it till you make it." How can you use "acting as if" to your advantage today? Where can you pretend a little to get you through the day?

DAY 30

LOOKING BACK AND LOOKING AHEAD

Big congratulations are in order because you've made it to 30 days of sobriety! It's a huge accomplishment, so please take a few moments today to really sit with what you have achieved. This is probably the hardest part of the recovery process, and you've made it through. Well done! It may be difficult to look too far down the road that lies ahead, but remember that you made it here one day at a time and you will continue to do so from here on out. If you can make it through your first 30 days of sobriety, you can probably make it through anything!

Keep in Mind

- You never have to do this again if you don't want to.

- You deserve to congratulate yourself on this accomplishment.

- Don't denigrate this achievement by comparing it to anything else. It doesn't matter what others may or may not be doing with their lives; 30 days sober is a huge milestone.

- You are strong, worthy, and capable even when it doesn't feel that way.

- You have the power and wisdom to keep going on this journey.

- It's okay if everything isn't better right now. It doesn't mean you've done anything wrong; it just means that it takes more than 30 days of sobriety to make progress on certain issues.

- There are still challenges ahead, and that is okay and normal.

Looking Back

Write down the most important thing that 30 days of sobriety has taught you about yourself. Did you surprise yourself in any ways? What are you most proud of at this point in your journey?

_____

_____

_____

_____

Looking Ahead

What goals do you have for the next 30 days, in addition to staying sober? How can you accomplish your goals for the next 30 days while also remembering to take things one day at a time? What lessons from your first 30 days can you take into your next 30 days?

_____

_____

_____

_____

A Disease of Forgetting

Alcoholism is a disease of forgetting. It tries to survive by making you forget how bad things got. You quit for a good reason, but given enough time alcoholism will have you thinking, "It wasn't *that* bad, was it? You made it a bigger deal than it really was." It may make you forget certain things entirely. Fight back against this forgetting by writing about all the reasons you've stopped drinking. What really happened? How bad did it truly get?

Co-Occurring Disorders

For some, alcoholism is their only mental health diagnosis. But others have both alcoholism and another mental illness, such as major depressive disorder, generalized anxiety disorder, panic disorder, bipolar I or II, post-traumatic stress disorder, borderline personality disorder, or schizophrenia. These individuals have co-occurring disorders, and a multiple diagnosis can make their recovery more complicated. If you've never been diagnosed with another disorder, do you suspect you may be struggling with something in addition to alcoholism? If so, whom can you reach out to for help figuring that out? If you already know you have another diagnosis, how is your newfound sobriety affecting your mental health recovery?

Shower Visualization

Do you ever feel like you're carrying around a bunch of heavy negative energy? Maybe you've generated this fog yourself, or picked it up from others, or a little of both. If you can relate, try doing this visualization exercise the next time you hop in the shower.

Use your imagination to see the cloud of funky energy in and around you. Stand under the showerhead and visualize the water working through and rinsing away the negative energy. Start at the top of your head, and go all the way down your body as the water flows. See the heavy energy melt off you and get washed down the drain to a faraway place where it cannot bother you again.

Willingness

Willingness is the quality or state of being prepared to do something. You were willing to stop drinking, and now you're here. Continued willingness will take you far in your recovery. What role does willingness play in your life today? If you're not yet willing to make certain changes, are you willing to become willing to make those changes?

This week I learned: _____

My biggest challenge was: _____

My biggest success was: _____

Self-Care Checklist

Y	N	
		Am I sleeping okay?
		Am I staying hydrated?
		Am I eating well?
		Am I moving around much?

TIP: *If you have trouble staying hydrated, get a water bottle or download an app that will remind you to drink water regularly throughout the day.*

This Week I Have . . .

○ Connected with another person.

○ Thought of things I'm grateful for.

○ Been kind and gentle with myself.

○ Stepped outside my comfort zone.

○ Taken direction from someone who knows more than I do.

I am staying sober because:

_____

_____

_____

_____

_____

_____

_____

_____

_____

_____

Relapse Is a Process

Relapses usually don't just happen. There is often some lead-up to the relapse itself, whether it's a series of events, a certain thought process, or a combination of both. Don't let your alcoholism blind you to the fact that you might be heading toward a relapse. Have you been in any risky situations lately, such as going out of your way to drive past your favorite bar or hanging around with people who are drinking to excess? Are you thinking about drinking a lot, or have you been looking back fondly on memories of drinking? How can you spot when you are getting close to a relapse?

_____

_____

_____

_____

_____

_____

_____

_____

_____

_____

_____

Box Breathing

Focused breathing exercises can help calm you down when you are anxious or craving a drink. Box breathing is a simple and easy one for you to practice today. To try it out, use a finger to trace along the lines of the box below as you breathe—one side for each step.

→ Inhale for 4 seconds.

→ Hold for 4 seconds.

→ Exhale for 4 seconds.

→ Hold for 4 seconds.

Repeat as many times as you need.

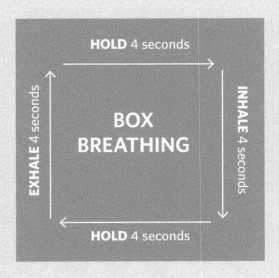

DAY 38

Identifying Triggers

What are your triggers for drinking? Are there certain activities, such as being around people drinking, going to parties, or being by yourself, that make you crave a drink? Do you get triggered when you hear people talk about drinking or see people drink in movies or on TV? Are certain emotions triggering for you? Do stress, boredom, joy, anger, fear, or excitement make you want to drink? It's important to identify your triggers because doing so can take the mystery out of why you sometimes want to drink. Then you're able to plan how to avoid and deal with your triggers more effectively in the future. List any triggers you can think of here.

Progress, Not Perfection

When you read the phrase, "Progress, not perfection," what does it make you think about your journey with sobriety so far? Even if things haven't gone perfectly, can you name three ways in which you have made progress?

Gratitude Practice

Focusing on things you are grateful for is a powerful way to get your head out of the dark and dangerous places alcoholism can take it. A gratitude practice is an important type of contrary action, which is when you do something you know is good for you even when you don't really feel like doing it. Let's give it a shot right now: List five things that you are grateful for today. They can be big or small, conventional or quirky. Afterward, reflect on how focusing on gratitude made you feel. Then establish a regular gratitude practice of writing down five things you're grateful for before you go to bed each night.

Values

Broadly speaking, we feel best about ourselves when we act in ways that bring us closer to our values. To do so, we need to know what our values are in the first place. Go through the table below and circle the values that are important to you. When you're done, put a star next to the top five most important ones. Write down that list of five and put it somewhere you will see it often so it can remind you to act in alignment with those values.

Acceptance	Flexibility	Love	Forgiveness	Intimacy
Freedom	Adventure	Responsibility	Cooperation	Persistence
Safety	Fun	Authenticity	Curiosity	Mindfulness
Justice	Connection	Integrity	Engagement	Sensuality
Creativity	Order	Honesty	Assertiveness	Friendliness

This week I learned: _____

My biggest challenge was: _____

My biggest success was: _____

Self-Care Checklist

Y	N	
		Am I sleeping okay?
		Am I staying hydrated?
		Am I eating well?
		Am I moving around much?

TIP: *Trust that your body knows when and how much it needs to eat in order to function optimally. Honor your hunger and fullness signals.*

This Week I Have . . .

○ Connected with another person.

○ Thought of things I'm grateful for.

○ Been kind and gentle with myself.

○ Stepped outside my comfort zone.

○ Taken direction from someone who knows more than I do.

I am staying sober because:

_____

_____

_____

_____

_____

_____

_____

_____

_____

_____

_____

Thinking and Acting

You can't think your way into right action, but you can act your way into right thinking.

—BILL WILSON, founder of Alcoholics Anonymous

Right now you are in a process of changing both your actions and your thinking. As Bill Wilson says, just thinking about changing your behavior isn't going to get you far. Changing your behavior, however, will start to improve your thinking. How have you already seen this play out after you stopped drinking? What is one other behavior you can change, and how do you hope changing that behavior will change your thinking?

_____

_____

_____

_____

_____

_____

Self-Esteem

Being a person with alcoholism, and doing the things people with alcoholism do when they're drinking, can strike huge blows to your self-esteem. A great way to build self-esteem is to do "esteemable" actions, such as being of service to others who are in need of help or taking care of yourself. Today, engage in five esteemable acts. Take note of how you feel about yourself after each one, and again at the end of the day.

Why Do You Drink?

Although every person with alcoholism has their own story, it has been said that people with alcoholism drink because they think they have to. Your relationship with alcohol has certainly evolved over time, and you've probably had various reasons you thought you had to drink. Why did you drink? Why might you still think that you have to drink?

_____

_____

_____

_____

_____

_____

_____

_____

_____

_____

_____

_____

_____

Recovery Isn't Linear

Many people expect sobriety and recovery to go like this:

But sobriety and recovery almost always go like this:

Write about the ups and downs you've experienced over the past 45 days. What have you learned from the fact that your recovery isn't exactly a linear process?

_____

_____

_____

_____

_____

_____

_____

Take What You Like and Leave the Rest

A saying in the rooms of 12-step programs is "Take what you like and leave the rest." This means you are allowed to use the information from Alcoholics Anonymous (AA) you find most helpful while also leaving by the wayside the parts that aren't useful to you. If AA is a part of your sobriety journey, how can you apply this saying to your experience with the program so far? If AA isn't something you're using at this time, can you still find value in this idea? Are there things you've learned in sobriety so far that you intend to take with you on your journey, and other things you haven't found helpful and will be leaving by the wayside?

Acceptance

Pain is mandatory, but suffering is optional. There is no such thing as a life without pain. Sure, some lives seem to have more pain than others, but no life is pain-free. Suffering, however, is when we refuse to accept pain. Then we've got two problems: the original pain, and the suffering caused by our refusal to accept it. Remember, just because you accept something doesn't mean you like it, agree with it, approve of it, or even understand it. It just means you are consenting to receive reality on reality's terms.

    Write about one recent experience you've had with refusing to accept pain in your life. How could things have been different if you had avoided the suffering caused by refusing to accept the pain?

This week I learned: _____

My biggest challenge was: _____

My biggest success was: _____

Self-Care Checklist

Y	N	
		Am I sleeping okay?
		Am I staying hydrated?
		Am I eating well?
		Am I moving around much?

TIP: *Are you a morning person or a night owl? If possible, adjust your sleep schedule to accommodate your natural circadian rhythms.*

This Week I Have . . .

○ Connected with another person.

○ Thought of things I'm grateful for.

○ Been kind and gentle with myself.

○ Stepped outside my comfort zone.

○ Taken direction from someone who knows more than I do.

I am staying sober because:

_____

_____

_____

_____

_____

_____

_____

_____

_____

_____

DAY 50

Religion, Spirituality, and Non-Spirituality

Some people recovering from alcoholism find it helpful to participate in a religious peer support group, such as the Christian group Celebrate Recovery. Others prefer support groups like Alcoholics Anonymous, which are spiritual but not tied to any particular religion. And still others find it most helpful to step back from religion or spirituality altogether. Which approach do you prefer? Have you tried the other options as well? What are the pros and cons of the path you have chosen?

Defusion

According to Acceptance and Commitment Therapy (ACT), we experience emotional pain when we fuse with (completely buy into and become one with) our inaccurate or unhelpful thoughts. ACT offers skills designed to help you defuse from such thoughts. Defusion isn't about getting rid of these thoughts, but rather getting some distance between you and them. Write down three thoughts you fuse with frequently. For example, *"I can't live without alcohol"* or *"Lifelong sobriety is impossible."*

_____

_____

_____

_____

_____

Now try the following defusion skills.

→ Start the thought with, "My head is telling me that . . . " So instead of "I can't live without alcohol," it's "My head is telling me I can't live without alcohol."

→ Label it as a story. "Here goes the 'I can't stay sober' story again!"

→ See your mind as a master salesperson trying hard to sell you a thought. Decide whether you actually want to buy the thought right now.

Insides and Outsides

In early sobriety you often feel like you're falling apart while those around you have their lives together. It is difficult to avoid comparing your insides to other people's outsides. When you do so you end up feeling bad because what others present on the outside often isn't an accurate reflection of what's going on inside.

The outline below is someone who seems to have it all figured out. On the outside, write what you see them presenting to the world. On the inside, write what might actually be going on for them internally. This exercise will help you see that not everyone is doing as well as they appear to be.

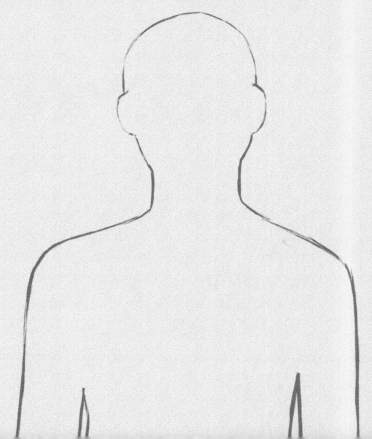

Being of Service

Being of service to other people is an excellent way to break the cycle of obsession with alcohol and self that can often dominate one's thoughts in early sobriety. It's also a great way to improve self-esteem. Write about one time you were of service to others and how it made you feel about yourself. Then write about three ways you can be of service to others over the next several days.

_____

_____

_____

_____

_____

_____

_____

_____

_____

_____

_____

_____

Sober Fun

If you drank for fun, or had fun while drinking, your alcoholism can often trick you into thinking that fun is not possible without alcohol. The reality is that sober fun can consist of literally any activity that doesn't involve (or have to involve) drinking—and that covers *a lot* of ground. Today, brainstorm at least five sober fun activities and commit to engaging in at least one.

Managing Triggers

Think back to the triggers you wrote about on Day 38. Now reflect on how you have been handling these triggers. Are you using techniques that help you ride the wave of the trigger successfully, or are you white-knuckling it and suspect that your next encounter with a trigger may lead to a relapse? Write about the last time you faced a trigger and what coping skills you used to handle it. If you feel like you were successful, explore how you can continue to face triggers effectively in the future. If you really struggled, write about three alternative strategies you can try next time that may be more effective.

DAY 56 CHECK-IN

This week I learned: _____

My biggest challenge was: _____

My biggest success was: _____

Self-Care Checklist

Y	N	
		Am I sleeping okay?
		Am I staying hydrated?
		Am I eating well?
		Am I moving around much?

TIP: *Exercise is healthy—in moderation. Don't swap addictions and replace excessive drinking with excessive exercise. Exercise addiction is real and harmful.*

This Week I Have . . .

○ Connected with another person.

○ Thought of things I'm grateful for.

○ Been kind and gentle with myself.

○ Stepped outside my comfort zone.

○ Taken direction from someone who knows more than I do.

I am staying sober because:

_____

_____

_____

_____

_____

_____

_____

_____

_____

_____

Disease or Choice?

Is alcoholism a disease or a choice? Alcoholism is a disease *of* choice. It is a mental illness that damages the areas of the brain used to make decisions about alcohol use. How have you seen this play out in your own life? How were the decisions you made about drinking different from decisions you may have made in other areas of your life?

_____

_____

_____

_____

_____

_____

_____

_____

_____

_____

_____

Opposite Action

Part of sobriety and recovery is doing the opposite of what you used to do—and what you may still feel like doing today. The most obvious example is not drinking even though sometimes you might still really want to. What are three types of opposite action you can engage in today to improve your recovery?

Do you really feel like isolating? Then you should probably:

_____

_____

Do you want to keep your urges to drink to yourself? Then you should probably:

_____

_____

Do you want to hang out with friends who drink heavily? Then you should probably:

_____

_____

Do you want to call an ex-partner who often upsets you? Then you should probably:

_____

_____

Do you want to skip that support group meeting? Then you should probably:

_____

_____

You can fill in others to address your specific needs.

_____

_____

Your Higher Power/Higher Purpose

Could a belief in a higher power or higher purpose help you in your sobriety? Are you aware of how many different higher powers or higher purposes you could believe in?

Jesus	God
Krishna	Mohammed
Buddha	Gaia
Hashem	The Universe
Nature	Love
Science	Honesty
Integrity	The list goes on!

How could it enrich your experience of sobriety to believe that one of these is a power greater than yourself that can direct you in life?

_____

_____

_____

_____

_____

_____

LOOKING BACK AND LOOKING AHEAD

You've made it through two months of sobriety. That's so amazing! This is such an important accomplishment—congratulations on getting to this point in your recovery. You've got 30 more days to go before you reach the milestone of 90 days sober. It may feel like a long way between here and there, but remember that you've already done it twice over. You've made it to such a crucial point in your sobriety, and this place can be the turning point for a whole new life. You are in the middle of building a sturdy foundation of balance, health, and authenticity.

Keep in Mind

- You are in the middle of a super important healing process, so give yourself some credit!

- You're allowed to rest and take in the magnitude of your accomplishments so far.

- You don't have to listen to your disease when it tells you that if you've made it this far, you can return to drinking and do it "like a normal person."

- You can be scared, uncertain, messy—and keep showing up for yourself anyway.

- You have the strength and willingness to keep going on this journey of a lifetime.

- Continue to be willing to listen to those with more experience in this area than you.

- Progress, not perfection.

Looking Back

Write down the most important thing that 60 days of sobriety has taught you about yourself. Did you surprise yourself in any ways? What are you most proud of at this point in your journey?

_____

_____

_____

_____

Looking Ahead

How can you accomplish your goals for the next 30 days while also remembering to take things one day at a time? What lessons from your first 60 days can you take into your next 30 days?

_____

_____

_____

_____

You Lose

The saying, "Whatever you put ahead of your sobriety, you lose" is a bit harsh, but it's also true. If you put your job ahead of your sobriety, sooner or later you will lose your job because you will not stay sober. The same is true of a relationship, finances, or any number of other things you might value. What is something you're putting ahead of your sobriety right now? How might it benefit you to take some contrary action and put your sobriety first?

Medication

Sometimes people recovering from alcoholism need to investigate whether non-addictive psychiatric medications can assist them in their recovery. Shame or stigma around psychiatric medications, or misinformation about how they work, shouldn't get in the way of this process. If you suspect you may need to be evaluated for medication by a psychiatrist, brainstorm how you can set this up. If you don't feel like psychiatric medication could help you in any way right now, write a little bit about three potential future warning signs that could indicate you should see a psychiatrist.

This week I learned: _____

My biggest challenge was: _____

My biggest success was: _____

Self-Care Checklist

Y	N	
		Am I sleeping okay?
		Am I staying hydrated?
		Am I eating well?
		Am I moving around much?

TIP: *Focus on drinking more water for hydration, and try to drink fewer coffees, teas, and caffeinated sodas that cause dehydration.*

This Week I Have . . .

○ Connected with another person.

○ Thought of things I'm grateful for.

○ Been kind and gentle with myself.

○ Stepped outside my comfort zone.

○ Taken direction from someone who knows more than I do.

I am staying sober because:

_____

_____

_____

_____

_____

_____

_____

_____

_____

_____

Resentments

Holding on to bitter indignation that you've been treated unfairly (aka resentment) will make you vulnerable to relapse. Use the sets of prompts on these pages to begin sorting through two of your biggest resentments. This exercise will make it easier to stop carrying them around with you. (Be sure to stay on the theme of resentments rather than more complex issues such as trauma, which should be treated with professional help.)

I'm resentful about . . .

_____

Because . . .

_____

What is my part in this situation?

_____

How does holding on to this resentment benefit me?

_____

How does holding on to this resentment harm me?

_____

(Continued)

I'm resentful about . . .

_____

Because . . .

_____

What is my part in this situation?

_____

How does holding on to this resentment benefit me?

_____

How does holding on to this resentment harm me?

_____

Turn It Over

One of the hardest parts of recovering from alcoholism is learning to let go of your ideas of what *should* be happening in your life. The more you cling to your will about these preconceptions, and the more you fight back against the realities of your life, the harder life becomes. Even though it can be very difficult to do, life becomes much easier when you turn your will, your shoulds, and your ideas over to something greater than yourself. On Day 59 you wrote about what this power is for you. Now write about how you can begin to practice trusting that this power might have different and even better things in mind for you than you could ever imagine. How can you turn yourself over to that idea?

Terminally Unique

Many people who struggle with alcoholism see themselves as "terminally unique"—totally unlike others who have a dependence on alcohol. They focus on all the ways they and their drinking are different, and the ways in which they don't fit in with the rest of the recovery crowd. This type of denial can be anywhere from risky to, well, terminal. Write about three ways you have seen or do see yourself as different from others who have a drinking problem. Then explore any areas of overlap between yourself and others with a drinking problem.

_____

_____

_____

_____

_____

_____

_____

_____

_____

_____

_____

Affirmations

Many people roll their eyes at affirmations, which is understandable given that they are often unrealistically positive. Affirmations are much more effective when they feel genuinely realistic and authentic. Below are a few affirmations that could be useful for newly sober people. Feel free to tweak them to fit your needs, and write some of your own, as well. Then find some way to say them to yourself multiple times today. Read them in front of a mirror, write them on a sticky note, or record yourself saying them and play it back a few times.

→ I can make it through the struggles of early sobriety.

→ I am willing to get back up again when I stumble.

→ I can ride the waves of cravings and come out sober on the other side.

→ I respect myself more every day.

→ One day I will be able to forgive myself for the things I did when I was drinking.

→ _____

_____

→ _____

_____

→ _____

_____

The Barbershop

Maybe you've been spending time around people who are drinking a lot, or engaging in some other behavior that potentially endangers your sobriety. So far, so good . . . you haven't fallen off the wagon. But keep in mind: If you hang around at the barbershop long enough, you're gonna get a haircut eventually. This is risky behavior for someone in their first 90 days of sobriety. Write about one way you've been "hanging around the barbershop" and how you can change this behavior to take yourself out of harm's way.

Simple, Not Easy

The act of not drinking is simple, but everything that comes along with it is not easy. It can be challenging to live in this paradox of something being both simple and hard at the same time. Write about three ways in which not drinking is a simple thing to do. Then write about three more ways in which not drinking is a hard thing to do. Finish by writing down your thoughts and feelings about what it's like to live in this paradox day to day.

DAY 70 CHECK-IN

This week I learned: _____

My biggest challenge was: _____

My biggest success was: _____

Self-Care Checklist

Y	N	
		Am I sleeping okay?
		Am I staying hydrated?
		Am I eating well?
		Am I moving around much?

TIP: *Restricting your dietary intake can lead to fatigue, overeating, and binges, so make sure you are eating enough food when you are hungry.*

This Week I Have . . .

○ Connected with another person.

○ Thought of things I'm grateful for.

○ Been kind and gentle with myself.

○ Stepped outside my comfort zone.

○ Taken direction from someone who knows more than I do.

I am staying sober because:

_____

_____

_____

_____

_____

_____

_____

_____

_____

_____

SMART Goals

Today, set a SMART goal for your sobriety journey. SMART goals help you map out a plan that is **s**pecific, **m**easurable, **a**ttainable, **r**elevant, and **t**ime-bound. Many people find these types of goals useful for staying accountable to themselves, rather than making vague plans or promises.

	Example SMART Goal	My SMART Goal
Specific	I'll connect with friends today.	
Measurable	I'll connect with five friends in some way (text, email, phone, etc.).	
Attainable	Well, maybe it should be two friends—that's more realistic.	
Relevant	They will be sober friends.	
Time-bound	I'll do it before 8 p.m.	

Your Hula-Hoop

In early sobriety, it's easy to get wrapped up in other people's dramas. Sometimes you do so because you miss the excitement and chaos that went along with drinking. Other times, it's a way for you to take the focus off your own recovery. Whatever the reason, try to remember that if you have a Hula-Hoop around your midsection, everything outside the Hula-Hoop is really none of your business. Another way to say it is, "Not my circus, not my monkeys." Write about a time over the past 71 days when you got overly involved in other people's drama. Explore the ways in which this behavior both benefited and hurt your sobriety.

Glimmers

Deb Dana, LCSW, used polyvagal theory (which posits that the vagus nerve plays a role in emotion regulation, social connection, and fear) to develop the concept of glimmers, which are essentially the opposite of triggers. Glimmers are things that cue our nervous system to enter a state of safety, calm, and groundedness. They can be experiences or things that help us feel safe and open the door to healthy connections with others and ourselves. You identified your triggers for drinking on Day 38, and now it's time to figure out what some of your glimmers are. Write about five things— people, experiences, resources, objects, and others—that make you feel safe, strong, and secure in your sobriety.

1. _____

_____

2. _____

_____

3. _____

_____

4. _____

_____

5. _____

_____

Shoulding

Dr. Albert Ellis, creator of rational emotive behavior therapy (REBT), originated the witty phrase, "Stop shoulding on yourself." *Should* is a word that typically creates only guilt, shame, envy, and resentment. So how about you try eliminating it from your vocabulary today? Whether you are speaking out loud to others or in your head to yourself, catch it and either eliminate it entirely or replace it with something else (see the example below). Each time you do this, and again at the end of the day, reflect on how not shoulding on yourself today made you feel.

Example: I shouldn't still be craving alcohol!
Replace should with: I'd rather not . . . , It would be better if I didn't . . . , I wish I didn't . . . , etc.

FEAR

There are many self-help acronyms for FEAR, but one that could help you most right now is:

FALSE

EVIDENCE

APPEARING

REAL

Early sobriety can be a fear-filled time, and this fear is often caused by false evidence appearing real. Because emotions run high during your first 90 days, it can be easy to let your mind convince you of things that aren't quite accurate. Instead of letting fears run rampant, take the time to see if they are, in fact, based on false (or distorted) information. Write about one of your biggest fears right now. Then explore whether it is based on facts, or if false evidence appearing real is really at the root of things.

Miracles

A miracle is a shift in perception from fear to love.

—A COURSE IN MIRACLES

Some people expect miracles in their first 90 days of sobriety. But miracles are often not grand, supernatural events. Sometimes a miracle is just a shift in perception—a seemingly small thing that actually has profound implications for someone's recovery. A shift in perception could potentially change the course of someone's life. Have you experienced any miracles in your first 90 days? If so, were they what were you expecting? Have you experienced any shifts in perception so far? If so, how have these shifts changed your life for the better?

_____

_____

_____

_____

_____

_____

DAY 77 CHECK-IN

This week I learned: _____

My biggest challenge was: _____

My biggest success was: _____

Self-Care Checklist

Y	N	
		Am I sleeping okay?
		Am I staying hydrated?
		Am I eating well?
		Am I moving around much?

TIP: *If you are still having trouble sleeping, it may be time to consult a doctor about non-addictive sleep medications or supplements that could help you get some rest.*

This Week I Have . . .

○ Connected with another person.

○ Thought of things I'm grateful for.

○ Been kind and gentle with myself.

○ Stepped outside my comfort zone.

○ Taken direction from someone who knows more than I do.

I am staying sober because:

_____

_____

_____

_____

_____

_____

_____

_____

_____

_____

Three for One

Every time you speak to yourself in a way that you would never speak to another person, say three kind things to yourself right afterward. It might feel like a lot of work at first, but every time you do so you create and strengthen new neural pathways in your brain that will help you change how you speak to yourself over time. The more you practice positive self-talk, the easier it will become.

Example: "Why am I so stupid! I can't believe I . . . wait, I'm doing it again. Okay, here goes: I'm 78 days sober. I took a shower today. I held the door open for someone at the grocery store."

Relapse Isn't an Eraser

Although counting sober time can be a helpful tool in recovery, one downside is starting your time over if you relapse. If it happens to you, remember that relapse does not and cannot erase the progress you made while sober. Nothing can take away the days, weeks, or months you had sober and the work you did during that time. Starting time over is a soft reset, not a hard one. If you have relapsed before, write about two positive changes you made while sober that relapse could not take away. If relapse isn't part of your story, write about how you can balance starting your time over with honoring your progress, should you ever relapse.

Boundaries

Boundaries are a difficult but necessary part of recovery. Because you can control only yourself, boundaries aren't about telling other people what to do; they are about what you are going to do.

→ Not a boundary: "Please drop drinking around me."

→ Boundary: "It's hard for me to be around you when you're drinking. If you drink around me again, I'm going to leave."

Setting a boundary is 50 percent of the work. The other 50 percent is holding the boundary if needed. Think of a boundary you need to set to protect your sobriety. Write out the boundary below, and then explore what might arise for you if you need to maintain the boundary. How might other people's responses to your boundary make you feel?

But & And

When we say "but," we are contrasting or negating what came before it. When we say "and," we are allowing everything to coexist equally. Try replacing your *buts* with *ands* today and see how that affects your thoughts and emotions. Here are some examples to get you in the flow of things.

Before: *"Sobriety has me so stressed, but I'm supposed to practice gratitude."*

After: *"Sobriety has me so stressed, and I'm supposed to practice gratitude."*

Before: *"I was doing so well today, but then I got hit by an intense craving to drink."*

After: *"I was doing so well today, and then I got hit by an intense craving to drink."*

Before: *"I need to connect with more sober people, but my social anxiety makes that tough."*

After: *"I need to connect with more sober people, and my social anxiety makes that tough."*

The Right People

By this point, you've probably learned that your sobriety won't scare away the right people. If someone disapproves of your sobriety so much that they distance themselves from you, was that really a person you would want close to you? If someone has such a strong negative reaction to your sobriety, it has a lot more to do with them than with you. Write about someone you may have lost along the way because they were put off by your sobriety. What does that person's disapproval of your sobriety mean to you now? Then write about three people in your life who have stuck around or maybe even gotten closer to you because of your sobriety. How are these relationships enriching your life?

Value-Neutral

Feelings are value-neutral. There are no good or bad, positive or negative, right or wrong feelings. Emotions can be pleasant or unpleasant, pleasurable or painful, but not positive or negative. How we decide to act on our feelings can be good or bad, but not the feelings themselves. What are your top three most pleasant feelings? What about your top three most painful emotions? What value judgments do you typically place on these feelings? Where did those judgments originate? Are they still serving you, or do they deserve to be revisited and revised?

DAY 84 CHECK-IN

This week I learned: _____

My biggest challenge was: _____

My biggest success was: _____

Self-Care Checklist

Y	N	
		Am I sleeping okay?
		Am I staying hydrated?
		Am I eating well?
		Am I moving around much?

TIP: *If intense cardio isn't your preference, look into slow and gentle types of movement like restorative yoga or tai chi.*

This Week I Have . . .

○ Connected with another person.

○ Thought of things I'm grateful for.

○ Been kind and gentle with myself.

○ Stepped outside my comfort zone.

○ Taken direction from someone who knows more than I do.

I am staying sober because:

_____

_____

_____

_____

_____

_____

_____

_____

_____

_____

_____

_____

Write a Letter

Think of someone you have a resentment toward. Write a letter to this person below. Make it free flowing and stream of consciousness, and don't censor yourself. You won't be giving this letter to the person, so really let them have it if you want to. Writing an unsent letter can be a useful way to help you process and let go of resentments that may be negatively affecting your recovery.

Inner-Child Work

We talked about one potential eye-roller on Day 67 (affirmations), and today it is time for another: inner-child work. If you can look beyond any negative knee-jerk reactions you may have to this topic, it could be a valuable recovery tool for you. If younger versions of yourself still existed somewhere inside your mind, do you think you could learn useful things about yourself from them? Might they have any valuable insights to share about your alcoholism and sobriety? Ask eight-year-old you a question and try writing the answer with your nondominant hand (the one you don't usually write with). Then ask them how it feels for you to be trying to connect with them. Their answers may surprise and enlighten you!

Peeling the Onion

Sobriety and recovery are like peeling the layers of an onion. You will always be uncovering deeper and more valuable information about yourself. Because you're getting close to 90 days, use the onion illustration below to show what layers you've uncovered so far. If the outer layer represents drinking, what inner layers have you uncovered? If you haven't gotten to the core of the onion yet, what do you suspect might be there? Two common options for what can be found inside the onion include depression and post-traumatic stress. Also, it's fine to put "drinking" on the outer layer of the onion.

Guided Meditation

Often when people say, "I tried meditation and I can't do it," it's because they don't realize succeeding at meditation doesn't involve stopping your thoughts. They don't understand that the work of meditation is in having your thoughts, and also having the willingness and focus to re-center them on the object of your meditation over and over again. *That* is meditation. Although meditation can be relaxing and grounding for many people, perhaps the most beneficial thing about meditation for those in early recovery is that it strengthens your brain's ability to shift focus. And a great type of meditation for non-meditators to start with is guided meditation. In this kind of meditation, you listen to a guide describe what you are supposed to be thinking of or visualizing for pretty much the entire time. Today, find a guided meditation to try. There are plenty of free guided meditations online, especially on YouTube. Even if the meditation is only five minutes long, give it a try and see if it's any better than your previous meditation attempts.

Just the Beginning

The first 90 days of sobriety are both a huge milestone and just the beginning. You've come to understand that sobriety alone isn't going to change your life. This journey has taught you that getting sober is the first step toward working on the underlying issues that drove you to drink. It's the turning point between sobriety and recovery. You're sober, but are you working to heal those deeper levels that drinking didn't let you access? Sobriety is great, but recovery is what will heal you and keep you sober. How can you use your first 90 days of sobriety as a jumping-off point into deeper recovery? What underlying issues need your attention now that you have been sober for three months?

LOOKING BACK AND LOOKING AHEAD

You've achieved 90 continuous days of sobriety! Wow, what a huge and wonderful goal to have reached. And some additional great news is that you never have to redo your first 90 days of sobriety if you don't want to. It would be nice to have to go through this only once, right? Even though there will certainly be struggles and stumbles ahead, odds are good that none of it will ever be as tough as what's behind you now. Here's to 90 more days, and then 90 more after that—one day at a time.

Keep in Mind

- Holy smokes, you did it!

- No, really: Sit with that for a little while and soak up the good vibes.

- No one and nothing, not even relapse, can take this accomplishment away from you.

- Hold in your heart and mind the fact that you didn't drink over any of the crises you faced during the past three months.

- Move forward with an open mind and remember that expectations are resentments waiting to happen.

- Be vigilant of your alcoholism trying to convince you that if you made it this far, you can drink again.

- Don't compare this accomplishment to what anyone else might be doing right now. This is a valuable success and you deserve to acknowledge and be proud of it.

- Remember to get back up if you fall down.

Looking Back

Write down the most important thing that 90 days of sobriety has taught you about yourself. Did you surprise yourself in any way? What are you most proud of at this point in your journey?

_____

_____

_____

_____

Looking Ahead

How can you accomplish your goals for the next 30 days while also remembering to take things one day at a time? What lessons from your first 90 days can you take into your next 30 days?

_____

_____

_____

_____

A Final Word

CONGRATULATIONS on making it through to the end of this guided journal! Hopefully you learned some things along the way that you can take with you on the rest of your recovery journey.

Using and completing this journal has put you on the path of deep recovery. As explored on Day 89, you have spent the past three months going beyond white-knuckling it through early sobriety. You have laid the foundation on which you can build a life of healing and balance. When people just focus on staying sober without doing any of the deeper work, they can become a "dry drunk." This (admittedly antiquated) term describes someone with alcoholism who focuses solely on not drinking and doesn't look at any of the underlying issues they drank over. These people are the definition of white-knuckling it, and are often unhappy and unpleasant to be around. It's an easy trap to fall into, and you deserve a huge amount of credit for avoiding it. Instead, by completing this journal and possibly doing additional work, you have begun to heal and recover on a much deeper level.

Where you go from here is simple, but not easy. Continue to stay sober one day at a time. Keep doing the hard work, peeling back the layers and healing what lies beneath. Try to strike a balance between pushing yourself beyond your comfort zone and knowing when to hit the pause button and rest for a bit. Reach out for help, connect with others, and remain teachable. Remember that you are a valuable and worthwhile human being just because you exist. You can do this. Just keep going.

Resources

RECOVERY PROGRAMS

Alcoholics Anonymous | aa.org
A 12 step–based peer support group that is spiritual but non-denominational.

LifeRing Secular Recovery | lifering.org
A secular peer-run addiction recovery support group.

Recovery Dharma | recoverydharma.org
A Buddhism-based peer support group for addiction recovery.

SMART Recovery | smartrecovery.org
Group addiction recovery support that is secular and science-based, using cognitive behavioral therapy and non-confrontational motivational methods.

FINDING A THERAPIST

Psychology Today | psychologytoday.com/us/therapists
The Find a Therapist search engine enables you to search by zip code, types of therapy, insurance, issues, and many other factors, and read a personal statement from each therapist.

SUPPORT GROUPS

ACOA | adultchildren.org
Support group for adult children of parents with alcoholism.

Al-Anon | al-anon.org
Support group for loved ones of people with alcoholism.

CoDA | coda.org
Support group for people with codependency.

SLAA | slaafws.org
Support group for people with sex and love addiction.

DIGITAL MEDIA AND TOOLS

Insight Timer App | insighttimer.com
This smartphone app (and website) contains a multitude of free audio guided meditations of all lengths and types. You can find a meditation on virtually any topic here, including many on recovering from an addiction.

Pleasure Unwoven | vimeo.com/ondemand/pleasureunwoven
A documentary by physician Dr. Kevin McCauley, who has recovered from addiction and does an excellent job explaining the details of how addiction works in the human brain.

USEFUL BOOKS

Trauma and the 12 Steps, Revised and Expanded: An Inclusive Guide to Enhancing Recovery by Jamie March. North Atlantic Books, 2020.

Co-Occurring Disorders Recovery Workbook: Strategies to Manage Substance Use and Mental Health Disorders by Dennis C. Daley. Herald Publishing House, 2011.

The Inner Child Workbook: What to Do with Your Past When It Just Won't Go Away by Cathryn L. Taylor. TarcherPerigee, 1991.

The Body Keeps the Score: Brain, Mind, and Body in the Healing of Trauma by Bessel van der Kolk. Penguin Publishing Group, 2015.

Intuitive Eating: A Revolutionary Anti-Diet Approach (4th Edition) by Evelyn Tribole and Elyse Resche. St. Martin's Essentials, 2020.

References

Dana, Deb. *The Polyvagal Theory in Therapy: Engaging the Rhythm of Regulation.* New York: W. W. Norton & Company, 2018.

Ellis, Albert and Robert A. Harper. *A Guide to Rational Living.* Chatsworth, CA: Wilshire Book Company, 1975.

Foundation for Inner Peace. *A Course in Miracles.* Novato, CA: Foundation for Inner Peace, 1975.

Harris, Russ. *ACT Made Simple: An Easy-to-Read Primer on Acceptance and Commitment Therapy.* Oakland, CA: New Harbinger Publications, 2019.

Neff, Kristin. *Self-Compassion: The Proven Power of Being Kind to Yourself.* New York: William Morrow, 2015.

Wilson, Bill. *Alcoholics Anonymous: The Australian Experience.* Arncliffe, NSW, Australia: General Service Board of Alcoholics Anonymous, Australia, 1995.

ACKNOWLEDGMENTS

A big thank you to Callisto Media and everyone there who assisted me with the creation of this book.

Much gratitude and love to my husband and all my friends for their support while working on this project.

Thanks to everyone on my professional and personal journeys who helped me gather the wisdom I was able to put into this book.

And I am so grateful to all the people recovering from alcoholism who I have had the pleasure to work with or know personally over the years. You have all given me such valuable insights and helped me become a better addiction professional.

ABOUT THE AUTHOR

Dr. Natalie Feinblatt is a licensed psychologist in Los Angeles, California. She earned her BA in psychology from the University of California, San Diego, and her MA and PsyD from Pepperdine University. She has been working in the mental health field for almost 20 years. Dr. Feinblatt has worked at all levels of care, from residential to outpatient, and is currently in private practice. She specializes in helping people heal from addictions and trauma. She has worked with many survivors of one-time or repeated physical, sexual, and relational trauma. A subspecialty of her trauma work is helping former cult members. She is trained in Eye Movement Desensitization and Reprocessing (EMDR), Brainspotting, Cognitive Behavioral Therapy (CBT), and Acceptance and Commitment Therapy (ACT). Dr. Feinblatt practices from a Health at Every Size and fat acceptance perspective, is LGBTQIA+ affirmative, and does not pathologize sex work, kinks, or ethical non-monogamy. Learn more and contact Dr. Feinblatt at DrNatalieFeinblatt.com.

CPSIA information can be obtained
at www.ICGtesting.com
Printed in the USA
JSHW051441121021
19512JS00002B/3

9 781648 764639

The First 90 Days of Sobriety:
Recovering from Alcoholism